So You Want to be in Government?

Handbook for Appointed Officials in America's Governments

Richard P. Nathan

The
Rockefeller
Institute
Press

Rockefeller Institute Press, Albany, New York 12203-1003
© 2000 by the Rockefeller Institute Press
Printed in the United States of America

The Rockefeller Institute Press
The Nelson A. Rockefeller Institute of Government
411 State Street
Albany, New York 12203-1003

Library of Congress Cataloging-in-Publication Data

Library of Congress Cataloging-in-Publication Data

Nathan, Richard P.
    So you want to be in government? : handbook for the appointed officials in America's
governments / Richard P. Nathan.
        p. cm.
    Includes bibliographical references and index.
    ISBN 0-914341-75-8 (pbk. : alk. paper)
        1. Government executives--Selection and appointment--United States. 2. Government
executives--United States. 3. Political planning--United States. I. Title.

JK761 .N29 2000
352.3'0973--dc21

                                                                00-051716

ISBN: 0-914341-75-8

To my Mother, Betty Nathan,
who contributed the title and
much more than that to this essay.

Contents

Acknowledgments

T his small book — really a long essay — is not meant as a contribution to the academic literature; nevertheless, I hope it will be read by, and of value to, students of American government, politics, and public affairs. I want to thank the many people who contributed to the ideas advanced and the advice proffered here. Two editors, Robert Cohen and Sandra Hackman, helped me craft this manuscript into what I hope is a user-friendly form. Carol Kuhl and Irene Pavone in my office at the Rockefeller Institute worked very hard revising the manuscript, checking it, and gathering source materials.

More than any other group, students I taught at the Woodrow Wilson School of Princeton University from 1980 to 1989 inspired me to want to write this *"How-to-do-it"* book about ways one can gain and use influence constructively as an appointed leader inside America's governments. I felt that we (the faculty — myself included) did not tell our students enough of what they needed to know about *how to govern* and lead in the public service. I kept my thoughts about this in a mental file, supplemented by reflections about experiences I had as an appointed federal official (U.S. Office of Management and Budget and Department of Health, Education and Welfare) and experience working as a Congressional aide and as a member and staff assistant to various federal and state commissions and advisory groups over the years.

The always-efficient Michael Cooper, director of publications at the Rockefeller Institute, assisted me in the preparation, and managed the production, of this essay.

1 Joining the "Governing Class"

Three classes of people work for America's governments. The first is *elected* officials. Close to half a million people serve as elected officials in the national government and state and local governments according to data collected by the U.S. Bureau of the Census.[1] The highest-level officials in this group are famous and visible public officials, often virtual media celebrities. The point I want to stress about the people in this most prominent group of public officials is that their time and energy typically are so dominated by high-hype media relations, campaigning, and political fundraising that they have little time left to make and execute public policies. British political scientist and long-time American politics watcher Anthony King notes that there are what he calls "never-ending" election campaigns in the United States. "In other countries election campaigns have both beginning and ends and there are even periods, often prolonged periods, when no campaigns take place at all." King observes further that in few countries "do elections and campaigns cost as much as they do in the United States," which is surely an understatement.[2] Some elected chief executives and legislators in the U.S. care greatly about, and are deeply involved in, the serious business of governing. But for most high-level elected officials the tasks of developing policies and managing government agencies are difficult to carry out while doing all the things they have to do raising funds and constantly campaigning to get reelected.

The second group of public officials is *career* government workers, civil servants who have tenure in their position. They are employed in national, state, and local civil service systems grounded in the merit principle. They also can be members of public-sector unions, which is the fastest growing area of unionization in recent decades. A major aim of both merit systems and public-sector unions is to shield career government employees from the constant political jockeying of elective politics. Workers in career positions like this constitute the great mass of America's 20 million public employees, most of them in local government.

This was not always the way it was. In the early days, all positions in American government were patronage jobs. This was the "spoils system." To the victors go the spoils. Getting rid of the spoils system by creating civil service jobs outside of politics was a hot-button political reform issue one hundred years ago, something like the way the issue of large campaign contributions is a high-salience issue now in American politics. Over the long haul, reformers prevailed but not all the way. At one point essentially all federal government jobs were appointive; now the great bulk of government jobs are protected civil service positions.

"The Governing Class"

However, it is this third group of people who work for America's governments, whom I refer to as *"the governing class,"* which is the subject of this book. These officials are *selected*, not *elected*. Although there are no data available on the number of people in this category, I estimate that somewhere between 350,000 to 400,000 people serve in national, state, and local governments in appointive positions. These officials do the heavy lifting of policymaking and management in America's governments. They play a significant role as change agents in the nation's political system. Yet this role is not well understood by the public, nor is it well described in the academic literature. Books about American government tend to focus on the highest-level elected figures — presidents, senators and other key legislators, governors, and big-city mayors. Although such figures dominate the political stage, if one really wants to understand leadership in American government, examining what the most high-octane elected officials do is by no means enough.

As government has grown and become involved in regulating and influencing more and more areas of our national life, so has the role of appointed officials, not just in Washington, but throughout the country. Altogether, the government expenditures account for 17.5 percent of the nation's gross domestic product; all governments (federal, state, and local) directly employ 15 percent of the nation's total labor force, most of whom are state and local employees. States and local governments do the main work of domestic government. We virtually could not live without them. They police communities; build, pave, and maintain roads and bridges; administer traffic safety, airports, and parks; collect trash; and assure the provision of pure water drinking. They are engaged in teaching, training, and counseling in public schools, universities, and community colleges. They staff prisons and administer the courts. They are responsible for environmental protection. They care for the elderly and administer programs to lift needy families out of poverty and into jobs, and they provide some poor families and also elderly people with subsidized housing. They operate public hospitals and provide health care for the indigent.

In recent years, as American politics has become high theatre dominated by prominent media clashes and personality issues, it tends not to be focused on what governments actually do and how well they carry out their purposes. In an ironic way, increased levels of controversy and the personality-focus of celebrity politics makes the unsung work of appointed officials in the nation's governing class all the more important.

The arrangements of government employees in other industrial democracies are strikingly different from those in the United States. Career tracks for top-level public-sector leaders are much more highly professionalized. A talented person who enters the British civil service ultimately can look forward to becoming a permanent secretary, which is the position in British cabinet departments just below that of minister. These positions typically are filled by graduates from elite preparatory schools and the most prestigious universities. In France, exceptional students admitted to *L'Ecole National d'Administration* can look forward in the same way to careers of high influence and responsibility in government. Although public policy graduate schools at American universities have tried (to their credit) to play a similar role in preparing exceptional students for high-level leadership careers in government, nothing like the British or French arrangements exist here.

The U.S. System

We know the most about appointed officials in the executive branch. Every four years, right after a presidential election, Congress publishes a so-called "Plum Book" (in some years it actually has a plum-colored cover) listing all appointive positions in the federal executive branch of the United States Government. Altogether, there are about eight thousand appointive positions in the executive branch. The quadrennial listing of these jobs in the "Plum Book" is the bible for people seeking to enter a new administration. Roughly the same number of appointed employees work for the U.S. Congress. There are even larger numbers of appointed officials, both executive and legislative, in state and local governments. All of these officials serve *"at the pleasure"* (the phrase is an important one) of whoever appointed them.

Being part of this governing class is not a career path. People in these positions enter, exit, and often reenter public service over the course of their professional life. Harvard professor Richard E. Neustadt is credited with coining the term "inner and outer" for this distinctly American arrangement by which people alternate between public positions and private life. When not in government, they may be lawyers, business executives, professors, journalists, and officers of hospitals, universities, or other nonprofit organizations. In fact, these "outer" periods are often seen as a time for former officials to regroup, to recharge their batteries, and frequently in the process to earn a higher salary than is possible in the public sector, thus enabling them to afford to return to public service if and when the political stars are so aligned.

The most important appointive jobs, those of agency heads and top policymakers, entail exciting challenges and can have a major effect on the society and the nation's economy. Such public service can produce a gratifying sense of accomplishment along with recognition and prestige. But there is more to it. Successful leadership in the public service and the professional contacts it involves can enhance the likelihood of landing a well-paid job after one exits government. Although this does not sound so noble, it has its good side. It enables the American governmental system to attract talented people to the public service who might otherwise never participate in government. These talented people come to understand the nation's political process up close and personal.

Appointed leadership in America's governments is not for the faint of heart. The politics of both getting appointed and engaging in public service are intense; however, the great appeal of appointive office is that, unlike elective public office, most of the people in these positions are not caught up all the time in political fundraising and battered by incessant, and often intense, high-profile personal issues. Still, one cannot succeed in government without being political. Interpersonal skills, a thick skin, the courage to take a stand, and the quickness of wit to defend it are essential qualities. It is exhilarating at the top, but it can also be nerve wracking. Successful appointed leaders have to have a keen intuitive sense of the constant bargaining of the American political process.

The Academic View

Academics do not like this high politicization of appointive leadership in America. They tend to downplay both its scale and significance, and they often advocate reducing the number and curbing the role and power of appointed officials. The National Academy of Public Administration periodically takes this position. In 1985, the academy warned that "in a country as heavily dependent as ours on in-and-outers as executive leaders, deficiencies in the appointments system pose a serious risk to public management." The academy maintained that

> The number of positions filled by political appointment has grown too large and must be reduced. The House Government Operations and Senate Governmental Affairs Committees should conduct a government-wide assess-

ment to identify and reconvert many of those positions where career executives have been replaced by political appointees.[3]

In his influential book *A Government of Strangers*, political scientist Hugh Heclo called appointed federal "birds of passage," noting that their most obvious characteristic is "transience." He called for "selectively centralizing, cutting, and pooling partisan appointments." Likewise, the 1989 Volcker Commission on the Public Service, chaired by former Federal Reserve Board Chair Paul A. Volcker, held that

> ... the growth in recent years of the number of presidential appointees, whether those subject to Senate confirmation, noncareer senior executives, or personal and confidential assistants, should be curtailed. Although a reduction in the total number of presidential appointees must be based on position-by-position assessment, the Commission is confident that a substantial cut is possible, and believes a cut from the current 3,000 to no more than 2,000 is a reasonable target.[4]

The Twentieth Century Fund Task Force on the Presidential Appointment Process reached a similar conclusion in 1996.

> Reducing the number of presidential appointments will improve the appointment process while simultaneously increasing opportunity, raising morale and enhancing the appeal of careers in public service. This reduction would be good for the president, good for appointees, good for the public service, and good for the country.[5]

There is no question that having large numbers of officials serve on a time-limited basis in America's governments entails costs. One cost is that people may leave government at precisely the point at which they have learned enough to be effective. This cost can be measured in terms of the time new leaders take to learn the ropes. It is the reason they sometimes act too slowly, too quickly, or unwisely. Another cost occurs when political hacks are selected for leadership posts in government, which unfortunately is not an isolated occurrence.

Despite these drawbacks, many of the nation's high-level appointed officials are more qualified for their roles and dedicated to them than most academic experts are willing to admit. Moreover, because academics do not approve of this arrangement, experts on public management have conducted relatively few studies of the uniquely American system of high-level appointed officialdom. However, when David T. Stanley and colleagues at the Brookings Institution studied 1,000 top appointed leaders from Franklin Roosevelt's presidency through Lyndon Johnson's, they found that the executives were a "well-qualified group."[6] Noting that these officials served for relatively short periods of time, the authors urged longer tenure. But they also said many of their subjects were "well prepared" because they had held previous governmental positions.

Another study of federal political appointees conducted between 1982 and 1985 by the National Academy of Public Administration said that despite calls to the contrary, the governing class is growing. The Academy reported a steady increase in the number of top-level jobs.[7] Political scientist

Linda L. Fisher commented that "our expectations about their qualifications have increased as well," pointing out that "we now expect political executives to be effective managers of large government bureaucracies."[8] Despite short tenure (an average of about two years for cabinet officials), Fisher reported a marked increase in the proportion of people who "came into their positions directly from some other position involving public service."[9]

A Debatable Assumption

The assumption that leadership jobs in government should be walled off from politics is a debatable one. The contrary argument can be made that leaders in American life (public, private, and nonprofit) tend to understand each other better in the U.S. than in other countries precisely because so many of them move back and forth between the governmental and non-governmental worlds. The fact that appointed officials gain first-hand familiarity with government activities in this way means that these citizens develop a close tie to political institutions, defusing the kind of "we-versus-they" attitude between government and the citizenry that can be dangerous to a social order. Another advantage of the existence of this distinctly American governing class is that when top officials want to change policy direction, they can often do so relatively easily (or at least more easily than officials in other political systems) simply by appointing a new person to a particular job.

In any event, appointed officials are intrinsic to the operation of America's governments. The tendency to downplay appointive leadership results in people who might be interested in the public service lacking an understanding of the number and character of such opportunities. Greater knowledge could stimulate more people — hopefully talented, dedicated, politically skilled leaders, both young and older — to consider appointive public service, to learn how to succeed in these jobs, and to think of public service as an important part of their life experience. This, in short, is my purpose, to impart the knowledge needed to consider appointive public service, and thus I hope encouraging more people to seek such opportunities.

Turnover at the Top

A newly elected administration faces a gray area in deciding which officials to replace and which to keep. Large public agencies, whether national, state, or local, often are staffed with experienced incumbent employees who are in appointive positions and can be removed and replaced when a new administration takes office. However, if retained, many of these officials can help a newly elected administration accomplish its purposes. Despite this fact, the pressure for a clean sweep is often great. Political operatives who gave their all to elect a new administration understandably want to obtain as many jobs as they can for themselves and their troops. Sensitivity is necessary to decide which experienced incumbent office holders will be so helpful to a new team that they should be retained. Good advice for newly elected executive branch officials is to go easy on revenge when there is a changeover of political parties and to build on agency strengths, or at least wait awhile to decide which politically vulnerable personnel should be asked to stay on, and which should be asked to leave. In fact, a good test of a new regime in American government is whether it blithely sweeps everybody out or shrewdly retains valuable holdovers.

Deciding which offices should be political and which should be career jobs is a challenge all across the U.S. governmental landscape. Federal agencies, and even more so states and local governments, vary in the breadth and depth of the politicization of the public service. Some state governments maintain a tradition of re-staffing new administrations wholesale. Others are more selective about the types of jobs that turn over with a change at the top. Generally speaking, smaller states, and even some relatively large states that have a "good government" tradition, tend to retain the most able senior agency officials, despite the fact that they may be serving in what are ostensibly political positions. Even in sensitive policy areas, there are examples of state officials who have served under multiple governors, sometimes governors with very different political ideologies. In the biggest states, however, this is rare. The practice there tends to be the same as the federal practice, everybody out, that is, every appointed official, when there is a changeover in the party in power.

Despite this instability of the American political process, people take, and indeed seek, high-level appointive posts. Their reasons are varied and hard to pin down. Most people in high appointive posts in government could not tell you themselves everything you might like to know about their motives for entering public service. They could not sort out the importance of the desire to serve versus the value of a government position as a stepping stone for opportunities in the future. The most successful members of the governing class strike a delicate balance between their private goals and their public purposes. Even when they are outside of government they maintain contacts (formal and informal) with the incumbent leaders of public agencies in the functional areas of their interest and expertise. Although career-planning calculations are common in people's decisions regarding whether and when to seek appointive office, the most respected appointed leaders are men and women who above all have a commitment to public service and are dedicated to the serious work of government.

Types of Inners and Outers

Because of the nature of America's governing class, it is essential that appointed leaders maintain a professional base. Lawyers are one of the main sources of appointed leadership. Law, in fact, is a good career choice for young people who want challenging occupational opportunities but are not sure what their career track should be. Lawyers who specialize in areas like transportation, the environment, energy, housing, foreign trade, or labor relations are logical people to fill policy jobs in government, especially if (as is true of many lawyers) they have ties to a political party or an elected leader.

Business executives also account for a large number of political appointees, because, like lawyers, they often develop special familiarity with a particular functional area of government and have ties to a political party or group. Other specialists, like journalists who serve as press officers and campaign consultants who serve as political aides, also move in and out of government, although usually not in the highest posts. Another major source of candidates for appointive leadership is academics. Although sometimes portrayed as motivated by higher goals, academics have as much to gain by being inners and outers as lawyers and business executives. Promotions, tenure, salary increases, publications, and royalties (not to mention public recognition, Oh fame!) can ensue from public life.

If I may be permitted a personal digression here, often the hardest part for an academic inner and outer is not getting in, but behaving appropriately as an academic after getting out. The temptation (and it is great) is to continue back in academe to play politics. New learned behaviors are hard to shake — to hunt headlines and advocate, not educate. Academics need an especially strong dose of self-control to play the role of inner and outer. The line between partisanship and scholarship, the latter of which entails (or at least in my view, should entail) teaching people how to think, rather than what to think, is not an easy one to draw or adhere to. This, I would argue, is not a reason academics should eschew government service. But it is a reason they should be vigilant in separating politics and scholarship in their teaching and research after they have served.

The Ethics of Influence

Most appointive officials spend their careers (both inside and outside of government) within a functional subsystem, sometimes called an "iron triangle" because it includes the appropriate executive branch official, the chair or senior members of the counterpart legislative committee, and the head of the relevant outside interest group. People move around within these political subsystems and in the process develop extensive, if uncodified, knowledge of how to operate in these special environments. One result of the existence of these kinds of organizational arrangements is that sometimes cozy relationships develop that present a challenge in maintaining integrity in public life. Appointed officials face pressure to build ties to an industry, academic discipline, or profession in which they used to work and/or may want to work upon exiting governmental service. People who are inside must of necessity keep in mind that sooner or later their bread will be buttered by people who are outside. This is not to say that integrity is out the window, or that the interests of the nation do not override such career and personal considerations.

Both legal requirements and practical considerations come into play in deterring officials from abusing the American system of inners and outers by obtaining special treatment for friends and former or potential future associates. Federal conflict-of-interest laws prohibit a former official for a period of time (usually two years) from dealing with "a particular matter" that the former official "knows or reasonably should know was actually pending under his or her official responsibility."[10] Of course, laws like this are not easy to enforce. After all, what is a "particular matter"? While temptations exist, and in past periods were yielded to as a standard operating practice of the "spoils system" in American politics, the tone and conditions of most U.S. governments today clamp down on abuses. Competing interests and the ubiquitous media exert constant vigilance. Democracy is supposed to give lots of interests a chance to exert influence, but always with a bright light being shined on whether this is done according to accepted rules and practices.

* * * * *

The remainder of this book presents what I hope is useful advice on how one gets to be an appointed leader in America's governments and how one wields power once appointed. Chapters 3 through 6 discuss specific aspects of appointive leadership in America's governments — team building, policymaking, implementation, feedback and evaluation, and the crucial subject of dealing with the media. The final chapter calls for broadening the talent pool of the people who serve as appointed leaders inside America's governments.

The purpose of this book is not to defend, or even take a position on, the arrangement whereby appointed officials exercise so much influence in America's governments. Rather, it is to encourage people to become appointed leaders in the public service. This is the way it is! I want to urge young people to think about their future on a basis that involves devoting part of their career to crucial and exciting leadership challenges inside America's governments in high-level appointive positions.

Notes

1   U.S. Bureau of the Census, 1992 Census of Government: Popularly Elected Officials, vol. 1, no.2 (Washington, D.C.: U.S. Department of Commerce, June 1995), p. v.

2   Anthony King, "Running Scared," *The Atlantic Monthly*, January 1997, p. 41.

3   National Academy of Public Administration, *Leadership in Jeopardy: The Fraying of the Presidential Appointments System* (Washington, D.C.: The National Academy of Public Administration, Nov. 1985), p. 28.

4   The Volcker Commission Report, *Leadership for America: Rebuilding the Public Service* (Lexington, MA: Lexington Books, 1990), p. 7.

5   The Twentieth Century Fund Task Force on the Presidential Appointment Process, *Obstacle Course* (New York: The Twentieth Century Fund Press, 1996), p. 9.

6   David T. Stanley, Dean E. Mann, and Jameson W. Doig, *Men Who Govern: A Biographical Profile of Federal Political Executives* (Washington, D.C.: The Brookings Institution, 1967).

7   The National Academy of Public Administration, *Presidential Appointee Project* (Washington, D.C.: The National Academy of Public Administration, 1985).

8   Fisher, Linda, "Fifty Years of Presidential Appointments" in *The In- and Outers: Presidential Appointees and Transient Government in Washington*, ed. G. Calvin MacKenzie (Baltimore, MD: The Johns Hopkins University Press, 1987), p. 1.

9   Ibid., p. 15.

10 Ethics in Government Act of 1978, *Title V – Post Employment Conflict of Interest*.

2 Getting to Be — and Being — a Leader

I n the first chapter, I talked about the desirability of understanding America's "governing class" of appointed officialdom so as to be able, if the stars are aligned politically, to enter public service in a challenging leadership role. The key phrase is "if the stars are aligned politically." You have to be at the right point in a career, knowledgeable about pertinent subjects, and politically positioned so that your ideas and values fit the times and the proclivities of appointing officials. This is not something you can plan with precision for the obvious reason that shifts in political preferences, values, and ideas can't be factored into your career planning in a precise way. You can be ready. You can make useful contacts and build networks that could aid you as a candidate for high office. You can serve in staff assistantships that hone your skills and help to add to your networking base. You can support candidates and work on campaigns. You can make the right moves if the right conditions emerge, but in the final analysis no amount of planning for opportunities in appointive office can assure you that you will be the right person, at the right time, in the right place, for the right job.

What I take from this is that hopes and expectations about being inside of government in a high-influence role shouldn't be overbuilt. I say this even though my main message is that more citizens — younger and older — should understand the nature of such roles and keep an eye out for opportunities for high-level public service. When that moment occurs, there are some things you as a candidate can do, and some you can't. There are no hard and fast rules, but there are ways to think about how you can be chosen.

Assume you are an aspirant with the skills, tools, and contacts for a cabinet or high-level subcabinet position as an agency administrator or top policy advisor. A new administration is being formed or for some other reason a major post in your field becomes open. What should you do? You can campaign, but this has to be done artfully. Leadership in public service is seen by observers, especially reporters (although they would rarely admit it), as a privilege one must earn without seeming to have worked hard to be selected. So how do you campaign for a job you really want?

You need to mobilize friends, urging them to write and call on your behalf. You need to let them know who they should contact and how they should explain why your experience and ideas would enable you to effectively tackle a particular new challenge inside government. You need to urge your supporters to talk to each other and share the feedback they receive with you. You should identify someone you know who has media experience to advise you about how to get mentioned in the press when a new administration is being formed or a key position opens up. I have heard of aspirants to appointive office hiring public-relations consultants to engineer a campaign for them, but as a general rule I think this approach is unwise and could backfire. Again, one must appear to be called to service.

There are also cases in which career officials bite the political bullet and move up to appointive jobs, which of course entails risk. The risk occurs when the job is done — i.e., when a new leader or administration comes into office that official needs to search for a new job, perhaps outside of government. This isn't always the way it works. Sometimes, such a person can "fall back" into a civil service rating. My experience, however, is that moving up and out like this is a good thing for leaders inside the permanent government with special skills who can and should move up the leadership ladder in this way when the time is right to do so.

The suggestions just made may sound too pat. The truth of the matter is that after an election, the first thing the winning candidate usually does is take a vacation, which is often both needed and deserved. Good as their intentions may be, candidates for elected office and their handlers and advisors are likely to have been so absorbed by the give and take of campaigning that, before an election, relatively little attention is given to forming a government after it. All the attention is focused on getting to form a government — not doing it.

One result is that when the people making selections for top appointive positions get around to it, time is short, pressures to make decisions are very great, and there emerges a frenetic, almost chaotic, system (actually, hardly a system at all). Getting your oar in as a candidate for appointment requires fast, adroit action without much opportunity for delicate maneuvering to get to the right people on the right basis. This situation is common, adding to the point made earlier that while you can be on the lookout for opportunities for high-level public service as an appointed official, you should not be unrealistic about whether you can work it out. A little stoicism is in order in those intense moments when a new administration is being formed, which is ironic, because my basic argument is that good people should come forward to serve, as this is of great value to the body politic.

Even if you succeed in getting named to a high-level job, this is by no means the end of the line of getting appointed. At the national level especially, the next steps can be frustrating, owing to the need to clear high-level appointments politically and with the Federal Bureau of Investigation. For the highest-level jobs, U.S. Senate confirmation also can add delays and produce frustration, and even beyond that, can produce the airing of personal matters in the confirmation process that can cause embarrassment. This is particularly true of the federal service, as most members of a new administration come from outside of government. There follows a process of close and intense scrutiny — closest when the confirmation process is controlled or heavily influenced by legislators of the political party that is out of power in the executive branch. The same point applies to large states and cities, although not so much for smaller state governments and local jurisdictions with a less politicized political culture, where the top executive positions are more likely to carry over or be filled by people from inside government.

In large jurisdictions (particularly the federal government and big states and cities), candidates for high appointive office and family members and friends have to be prepared for often shrill opposition tactics to embarrass a candidate by revealing information about private finances and business and professional transactions and relationships that, while perfectly legal (otherwise stay clear of public office), raise questions about a candidate's fitness for office. Legislative confirmation processes can go overboard, but at the same time the scrutiny they involve is useful so the public can be assured of a candidate's integrity and sense of fairness. Confirmation processes also serve as a way to identify the kinds of issues on which the behavior of a particular public official should be watched most closely.

Which Political Party?

Despite the fact that both major parties encompass a broad ideological spectrum, Republicans and Democrats have a sense of obligation to their own kind. Thus, routes to public service often involve networks of acquaintances and colleagues which are partisan. Once adopted, a partisan identification is like glue. It sticks to you. It is not smart to change parties; it makes a statement about your reliability, and in politics reliability has a high premium. Nobody likes a turncoat.

Hence, a major decision for people who aspire to public service concerns which political party to join. Ideology is obviously a factor, although it is not the whole story. Family ties are another factor that draws people to a particular political party. Young people interested in politics often have life shaping experiences working in campaigns.

While party identification is important, your reputation in a substantive public policy area is often more important. People who are experts on finance, economics, the environment, agriculture, urban affairs and housing, health, welfare, or transportation, etc. are attractive to government leaders looking for help. One's reputation usually encompasses a particular view of the world, for example, pro-environment or pro-growth, in favor of or skeptical about measures to aid the poor, views that send a signal that politicians know how to receive. Your public identity, both political and substantive, can help you get in the door, but what do you do once you're inside?

Being Political

While you need to be known as substantively knowledgeable in order to achieve political influence, once you have power there is no substitute for skill in wielding it. Good citizenship and political power go together. Although many appointed leaders serve because of their commitment to their country and their community, those who succeed do so because they also have political skills or because they learn on the job how to be effective politically.

There is no one way of conducting yourself inside government. You can't be too standoffish and you need to be thick skinned. People in leadership positions in American government operate in a cauldron of constant jockeying focused on making and implementing policy. It is important to be bold when the occasion demands it, because in many situations fine calibrations of strategy are ignored in the give-and-take of policymaking. Knowing when to hold and when to fold is a valuable political sixth sense. Experienced players also know when it is smart to take a radical position so the action will come to them. They also know when the better course of action is to bargain incrementally.

Bear this in mind too: Sometimes you have to make deals on unrelated matters, supporting a program in one area to get someone's help in another, or agreeing to a project or to appoint someone to an office to win a legislative vote on a wholly different matter. It would be naïve and unwise to enter high public office (and many private positions as well) if you are unwilling to do some horse-trading to achieve goals you care about. But of this be certain: Get your fair measure. Also, avoid bargains you can't follow through on, and be careful not to make your reputation purely and simply as a deal-maker as opposed to being a person of substance and principle, standing for policy goals and ideas you care about.

Experienced hands in leadership positions inside government learn, or know intuitively, how to relate to crucial groups in the governmental process in ways that can advance their purposes. One generalization that almost always is helpful is: Give credit to others — that is, give credit rather than take credit. To plant an idea with legislators about something they can take credit for is often the best way to accomplish one's purposes. For example, telling a legislator (federal, state or local) about a new project or program that a member has been working on, and adding that a reporter is going to call later in the day to talk about it, can be the key to building a coalition for carrying out your chosen purposes. A successful former state agency director commented to me that this kind of base building — on a bipartisan basis — accounted for one third of his time. The general point, which is stressed throughout this book, is that cultivating trust and sharing credit with key groups (here I have in mind legislators, the press, officials in other agencies, top officials in your own agency) creates a form of political currency that is of inestimable value in the governmental process.

Although appointed leaders need to be intuitive about political bargaining and interpersonal relationships, one piece of advice I can give may provide some comfort. When a person takes on a new position, there is initially the luxury of having a honeymoon period. This period presents an opportunity to ask dumb questions. It is a period when the new officeholder should talk to a lot of people. This includes people in your agency, in other governmental jurisdictions, and in agencies with related missions, as well as customers (the organizations and individuals affected by your agency's activities). Good listeners are a rare breed in politics, but a smart one. During this honeymoon period you can gauge the lay of the land and shape your approach to new tasks. There is no substitute for the feel you get in this way — from looking around when you take charge. Even if a person held a prior position in the same agency or jurisdiction, once named to an office the leader must develop a new perspective on each new set of responsibilities.

The length of the honeymoon varies. In a crisis, it will be short. But, whatever its length, once the honeymoon period is over, it is really over! Then, your dumb questions become exactly that — dumb questions. At that point, the time for action is hard upon the new leader. Generally speaking, you should strike while the iron is hot. Do the tough things early. As time goes by, you will acquire baggage and develop strained relationships. Taking advantage of the excitement of a new start is a good strategy for making your mark.

There are always caveats. Despite what I just said about it being wise to stake out major policy directions early, not every question has to be decided when it is raised. Knowing when to act and how to wait until the right moment to act is intuitive for many people, but it also can be learned on the job by thinking about the timing of major decisions carefully and patiently. Major decisions do not so much take time as require astuteness about when the time is right to act.

The use of time — both early on and over the course of one's tenure in an appointed post — is an important subject in and of itself. Near-term time (an hour, a day, a week) is often portrayed by leaders in government, both elected and appointed, as hectic and frenetic — never offering a moment to think or reflect. This may be a good impression to give to outsiders so you can move on to the next subject or person, but it is not an indication of wisdom or good practice if it is actually and always the way you think and act.

The worst thing a leader can do is to be in such perpetual motion that wise decisions on important matters at the right moment are sacrificed to dealing with petty matters that are better left unattended or delegated to others. Jimmy Carter's practice of deciding who should use the White House tennis court and when they should play is often cited to make this point. Carter, formerly the commander of a nuclear submarine, was said to be a detail person. Some observers of his presidency believe this trait contributed to his lack of achievements in office. Although I think this characterization is overdone, the point about the importance of not being eaten up by details is critical. Inside the tornado, even if the impression you give to outsiders is that it is always stormy, you should be calm. Or at least try to be. And you should stay focused on the big issues.

Skill in handling interpersonal relationships is also critical for successful leadership inside government. The academic literature on public administration tends to argue that political leaders should always be nice. As a general rule, it is best to let people down easily, an iron fist in a velvet glove. Nevertheless, although gentleness, persuasion, and being considerate of others can win the day in many situations, a leader who does not recognize when the time is right to discipline subordinates is bound to learn the hard way that at critical moments the courage to act must not be sacrificed to the desire to be nice. Shy flowers wilt in American politics. Being firm can include taking strong action — i.e., expressing great concern about a particular problem or the way a particular matter has been handled. But a good rule of thumb about doing this is never to do it when you are really upset. It is okay to let people think you are angry, but it is always wise in a group situation to be sure that what is actually involved is cool, controlled anger.

Four hundred years ago, Niccolò Machiavelli put his finger on the relationship between leaders and their associates: "When you see the servant thinking more of his own interest than of yours, and seeking inwardly his own profit in everything, such a man will never make a good servant." On a positive note he added, "to keep his servant honest the prince ought to study him, honoring him, enriching him, doing him kindness, sharing with him the honors and cares."[1] Surely, this is right. Personal gestures and kindnesses are an important part of leadership. Even casual motivational gestures to people who depend on you can be instrumental and should be deliberate and purposeful. Different people require different strokes — both motivational and disciplinary. Some people need lots of stroking and thrive on it, while others need more mystery in their life. One of the important intuitive skills of being a leader is recognizing what makes people tick, how they can be motivated to work loyally and productively with you.

What makes a particular team member perform effectively is not the same at all times and in all situations. Moods and conditions matter. You also need to be sensitive about your own mood. If you are upset or tense, you need to be careful not to overreact when an associate makes a misstep but is a person you need over the long haul. No one is immune to mistakes and bad moments. This is not to say that it is always right to forgive. The people on your close-in support team, as discussed in the next chapter, ought to be disciplined if things are going badly, and if that doesn't work, they should be removed. Firings, however, should be rare. In fact, they can be a sign of unwise selections, or even of failed leadership.

Besides exercising strength when needed, appointive leaders can sometimes secure an advantage by being unpredictable. You need to be sure the action comes to you on matters of consequence, and that your staff and subordinates think in these terms. There are occasions when the impression you give to members of your staff is that their well-being is among your highest priorities, but that is not always what they should think. A little mystery, as I said, can be functional. Overall, the people around you need to know that you care greatly about their good performance in fulfilling _your_ purposes, and that when it is necessary you can take strong and direct action with people who stray too far from these purposes.

Loyalty

Leaders frequently talk extravagantly about other leaders they respect, suggesting that they will always do the bidding of these colleagues, whether they be legislators, officials in other agencies, or leaders of important institutions or organizations outside of government. Such statements, however, often are not a full and honest reflection of what a leader really thinks. That is because loyalties shift both in time and over time. Stroking, even flattering, people you have relationships with can be very useful, but you need to keep in mind that different strategies and degrees of stroking are needed at different times for different people and on different issues. These calculations, too, are intuitive. It is often the case that a leader is not sure herself what the direction and degree of loyalty should be in a particular situation. This is especially so in intense periods when events are moving rapidly and alliances are shifting. Overall, calculations about loyalty not only have to be self-consciously changeable, they also have to be private. You can be loyal to your chief on some issues, but not others, at some times, but not others, in some settings, but not others.

Political scientist James Q. Wilson wrote this way about loyalty at the top in American government:

> A remarkable transfiguration occurs at the very moment a president administers the oath of office to cabinet secretaries or bureau chiefs. Just before the appointees place their hand on the Bible they are committed followers of the president's principles and policies. The oath uttered, the hands are lifted from the Bible; almost immediately, the

oath takers begin to experience a soul-changing conversion. Suddenly they see the work through the eyes of their agencies — their unmet needs, their unfulfilled agendas, their loyal and hard-working employees.[2]

Likewise, Harry Truman is reported to have complained, "I thought I was the president, but when it comes to these bureaucrats, I can't do a damn thing." Presidential scholar Clinton Rossiter speculated that many a president would have considered his hardest job "not to persuade Congress to support a policy dear to his political heart, but to persuade the pertinent bureau or agency — even when headed by men of his own choosing — to follow his direction faithfully and transform the shadow of the policy into the substance of the program."[3]

The U.S. Constitution hedges on the strength of executive leadership. Article II vests "executive power" in the president, yet other provisions assign powers to Congress in ways that water down this authority. Congress has used its constitutional authority to vest power "in the heads of department" to assign statutory authority to specific officials at or below cabinet rank rather than to the president. In his classic study of the presidency, Edward S. Corwin referred to the words "executive power" in Article II of the U.S. Constitution as a "term of uncertain content."[4] A president's, governor's, or mayor's relationship to executive branch agencies depends not so much on the law as on his or her own strength, strategy, and constituencies.

Every modern president has created management advisory groups. In characteristic fashion, President Lyndon B. Johnson's council on organization and management operated in secrecy, but its report pulled no punches in diagnosing the problem.

> Top political executives — the President and Cabinet Secretaries — preside over agencies which they never own and only rarely command. Their managerial authority is constantly challenged by powerful legislative committees, well-organized interest groups, entrenched bureau chiefs with narrow program mandates, and the career civil service.[5]

This reality of constantly shifting loyalties is reflected in perennial dilemmas of leadership for appointed officials at all levels. It puts a premium on working wisely and well with a wide range of people and groups, including particularly members of one's own staff and parallel leaders (that is, colleagues at your same level, such as other cabinet or subcabinet officials). This subject of building and working with a leadership team of staff members and also with other appointed leaders is taken up next.

Notes

1   Niccolo Machiavelli, *The Prince* (Ware, Hertfordshire, UK: Wordsworth Editions Ltd, 1993), p. 182

2   James Q. Wilson, *Bureaucracy: What Government Agencies Do and Why They Do It* (New York: Basic Books, 1989), pp. 260-261.

3   Clinton Rossiter, *The American Presidency* (New York: New American Library, 1956), p. 42

4   Edward W. Corwin, *The President: Office and Powers*, (New York: New York University Press, 1957), p. 3.

5   President's Task Force on Governmental Organization, "The Organization and Management of Great Society Programs, Final Report of the President's Task Force on Governmental Organization," June 1957, p. 6. Administratively confidential, unpublished.

3 Team Building

I n this chapter, I draw a distinction between two types of
leadership teams, for ease of exposition called the
A-Team and the B-Team. The A-Team consists of people parallel to an appointed leader, such as cabinet or
subcabinet colleagues. The B-Team is the leader's support
team. I focus first and most of all on the B-Team, because
forming it is a crucial early step for all political appointees and
because appointed leaders usually have the most discretion in
selecting and deploying their top aides and advisors.

The B-Team

The word "team" suggests a group of people who share a
knowledge of plays. A team should consist of a manageable
number of people who work closely and well together on a regular basis. Experts on management write about "span of con-

trol" — the point being that a leader can work regularly with a limited number of associates. There is no magic number. Maybe it is seven, maybe ten, but more than a dozen becomes problematic.

The three main criteria in selecting members of your support team are: point of view, chemistry, and balance. Other criteria include intelligence, experience, and interpersonal skills, but those attributes are givens for associates in all leadership settings.

The most important attribute an appointive leader must consider in forming a close-in support team is *balance.* Far and away the worst mistake you can make is to choose all one kind of associate. The wise leader knows that inputs from different types of people are essential — for example, from a political expert, a brainy type, a public-relations type, a hardball type, a compassionate type. Also factored into this mix should be people from different generations with different backgrounds and prior experiences. One person can bring several qualities and perspectives to bear — a young person with a Ph.D. in economics who previously worked at a different level of government, for example.

At critical moments, if everyone around you is too hard boiled or soft boiled, too analytical, too legalistic, or too political, mistakes are likely to occur. If your support team consists entirely of public-relations types, the group can be too shallow. If team members are all policy experts, they are likely to lack political skills.

A well known example of how an unbalanced support team can misfire is President Nixon's circling of the wagons to protect himself during the Watergate investigation. His team of close-in advisors was composed almost entirely of political operatives. No one with a sense of history or deep experience in other institutions was part of the inner circle. Bad traits reinforced each other, and wrong decisions were made until there was no way out.

The other two critical attributes for selecting B-Team members are point of view and chemistry. As to the former, if someone has a decidedly different point of view and values and goals than you, he or she is not likely to be a good B-Team member, no matter how talented. It is good to know the views of the other side, but a close-in associate too wedded to these views can disrupt decision making in ways that are dysfunctional.

The term *"chemistry"* refers to the elusive quality of people who relate comfortably to you as the leader and to each other. Good chemistry sometimes involves people with similar personalities. It can also involve people with different qualities who fit together well. Some leaders are intense, impatient, humorless; they may work well with support-team members who are relaxed, patient, funny.

If a leader has a high enough position, many B-Team members are likely to be people the leader chooses. The appointee can tap people inside of government, former associates from outside, or other outsiders recruited because of their experience or special knowledge relevant to the leader's goals.

Complications arise if someone other than the leader se-
lects B-Team members or has to approve their appointment,
but even a very high-level appointee rarely has full discretion
in forming a support team. This is partly because at least some
members are likely to be in permanent jobs as civil servants.
They were there before you, and they will be there after you
depart. They can wait you out. However, this is not an insur-
mountable obstacle. The new appointee should not be categor-
ically suspicious — as too many political types are — of all
civil servants, assuming they will be uncooperative and that
their perspectives, values, and goals are different from yours.
If you inherit careerists around you upon taking office, it is a
good idea to let a little time elapse before deciding whether a
particular person should be moved or removed, assuming that
you have the authority to do this.

The civil service is usually not so rigid that people cannot
be motivated or moved. Civil servants are evaluated regularly
for reassignments as well as raises and rewards. Most of the
highest-level career officials in the federal government are
members of the special corps called the "Senior Executive Service."* They have to be canny politicians in their own right because they can be moved around, even removed, much more
easily now than in the past. This arrangement empowers ap-

---

* The Senior Executive Service was established by the 1978 Civil Service
  Reform Act under President Jimmy Carter as a "good government"
  reform. However, some management experts think it backfired because it
  ultimately gave more power and prominence to appointed officials.
  Reagan's administration, which succeeded Carter's, used this authority
  in ways that enhanced the power of cabinet and subcabinet officials.

pointed officials. It needs to be seen as another way in which the American governing class of appointed officials has a special character and a strong role.

Inners and outers invariably also have to work well and wisely with many members of the permanent government. Despite reservations appointed officials may have about careerists, they need help and support from many of them. Civil servants know the rules and the ropes. Their knowledge of the laws and regulations that define how governments conduct their business often is a crucial ingredient to success. A good example is contracting.

Much of what modern governments do today is done through contracts with private companies and nonprofit organizations. Contracting laws and procedures may seem arcane, slow, and needlessly complex. Nevertheless, appointed leaders have to be sure they are well advised on what is possible and permissible in selecting contractors and overseeing their work. Friends and contributors often seek business from government, and indeed their bids may be the best ones you receive. But you need to be sure. In some cases, you may need to recuse yourself from the selection process. There is no substitute for developing trusting working relationships with civil servants who can protect agency heads and help them make sure they are following proper contracting procedures.

There is of course another side to this relationship. No matter what their status (whether or not they are members of the Senior Executive Service) career officials have many reasons for wanting to work effectively with political appointees.

One reason may be that they agree with the appointees. Another reason may be that civil servants care about the reputation and smooth functioning of their agency. Still another may be that appointed chiefs have leverage — some of it subtle, and some less so — such as the ability to assign career employees to remote branch offices.

The A-Team

The A-Team consists of people with parallel jobs, as, for example, the president's or a governor's cabinet. In describing the A-Team, we need to be careful about the "team" metaphor, although it is basically useful. Depending on the style of a particular elected chief executive, the cabinet may not be a team in the sense that its members meet frequently and work together closely. But they are nonetheless usefully viewed as a group. Inept cabinet making can undo a political chief executive in ways that may never be correctable.

Although the same three criteria apply to the selection of members of the A-Team as to the B-Team (balance, point of view, and chemistry), their ranking differs. While balance is the most essential criterion for the B-Team, a chief executive's foremost criterion in choosing cabinet-level and other top officials should be compatibility of point of view. In American government, alliances are evanescent. Today's collaborator may be tomorrow's adversary. Because of this, it is important to seek as much point-of-view compatibility at the top as possible, despite the tendency in American political practice to do just the opposite.

Because agency heads are pulled in so many different directions and are so highly influenced by stakeholders in their particular policy arena, there is bound to be trouble if the goals they care about are decidedly different from those of their chief. Under such conditions cabinet members are likely to build their strongest alliances with other power centers, such as legislative committees, interest groups, corporations, unions. There are huge temptations to do this. The executive branch of an American government (federal, state, or local), never a cohesive entity, is likely under these conditions to become a collection of unhappy people whose relationships with their chief and with each other are decidedly strained, even antagonistic.

Some readers may find the caution to avoid fractious cabinet making exaggerated, but habits die hard in American government. Elected chief executives often choose ideologically diverse cabinets. Most presidents, governors, and mayors, etc. are elected by coalitions of organizations and voters representing a mix of ideas and aims. Moreover, most elections tend to be won at the center of the ideological spectrum, and the center by definition is squishy. Hence, an eclectic approach (one liberal, one conservative, etc.) to cabinet making may seem logical — but it isn't. There is political wisdom in avoiding campaign payoffs (even legitimate ones) by not choosing cabinet members who are more beholden to other drummers than to their chief. It is difficult enough to maintain policy cohesion amidst the hyper-pluralism of American government. A strategy that gives up the game before the kickoff is very unwise.

The Sub-Cabinet

For purposes of this book, it is the next level of appointments that is most important. Presidents, governors, and chief executives of large cities and counties need to have a strong hand in choosing the members of their cabinet and their own personal close-in support team (the B-Team). Although some portion of the latter task can be delegated to a chief of staff, it is not a good idea to delegate too much of that responsibility, as the person who chooses the members of the White House staff or a governor's top aides is likely to win and hold those appointees' loyalty. However, not everyone appointed to the sub-cabinet (undersecretaries, assistant secretaries, agency heads, etc.) must be or should be selected by the elected chief executive. Which subcabinet appointments should be made centrally by the elected chief, and which ones should be delegated to top-level appointees?

There are pulls in both directions. On the one hand, making these appointments centrally enables the elected chief to achieve point-of-view compatibility. If the director of, say, the highway department, which is part of the department of transportation, is chosen by the governor, one would expect decisions about major highway routes to be in line with the governor's policy preferences and political needs. But on the other hand, if the cabinet secretary who heads the transportation department does not have at least some hand in this selection process, it is hard for the governor to hold that cabinet secretary accountable for policies and programs.

No single approach to choosing sub-cabinet appointees is right for all seasons. Elected chiefs can establish tight clearance procedures for all such appointments or delegate all of them to their senior appointed cabinet members. It is unlikely, however, that an elected chief would take such an all-or-nothing position. Even for delegated sub-cabinet appointments, it is wise for the elected chief to maintain a vetting or consultative process involving the elected chief executive and/or his or her top aides. Likewise, for sub-cabinet appointments that are centralized, it is wise for cabinet agency heads to be consulted about the choices made.

One more point needs to be added here. Team building at the cabinet and sub-cabinet levels is not a one time thing. Personnel changes have to be made all along the way.

Although I hope the observations made in this chapter involve ideas that can help appointing officials think about ways to facilitate and smooth out appointment processes, both for the highest-level cabinet and subcabinet positions and support teams, it needs to be stressed that frictionless government is not the American way. Shifting alliances are built into U.S. governmental processes, including the critical areas of choosing political appointees. Everything an appointed official can do to assure good working relationships by operating astutely and skillfully with others in the appointments process will make it easier, once a government is formed, to operate in all of the other bargaining arenas that are intrinsic to the unrelenting pulling and hauling of democratic government in the United States.

4 Making Policy

T here are many reasons for seeking public office. Some are substantive, which are the reasons highlighted in this chapter. A quick way to state my purpose here is to ask: How does a leader inside of America's governments go beyond vague campaign promises to decide which goals to pursue and how to pursue them? The policymaking process has many parts. This includes influencing the legislative process, responding to legal challenges, interpreting the legal basis for administrative action, issuing regulations and policy guidelines, and appointing other high officials, all of which require constant decision making regarding goals and strategies. Two social science disciplines, economics and political science, are juxtaposed in this chapter to discuss important intellectual underpinnings of the policymaking process.

Macroeconomics, the study of how economies operate in the aggregate, exerted its greatest influence in the U.S. federal government in the Kennedy period in the 1960s. The Kennedy administration drew on the writing of John Maynard Keynes to devise a program to achieve non-inflationary economic growth by cutting taxes in order to avoid "fiscal drag" and enable the economy to operate at full capacity. Later, in the Johnson years, microeconomics, the more detailed study of economic behavior, came to exert a similarly strong influence inside government. This chapter emphasizes the application of microeconomics in government, drawing heavily on the effort under President Johnson to highlight microeconomics in budgeting.

The Budget Process

The budget process is the spinal column of public policymaking. It is essential that appointed officials study it closely and participate in it. Appointed officials often enter government with only general ideas about budgeting. But, like it or not, they soon will be caught up in the budget process if they are trying to make a difference.

One influential school of thought about governmental budgeting is derived from political science, and is best reflected in the writings of Charles E. Lindblom, who was actually an economist by training. Lindblom published a seminal article in the *Public Administrative Review* in 1959 called "The Science of Muddling Through." He began by noting there are two ways to solve complex policy problems, by root and by branch. The root approach looks at the whole. It is grounded in theory, examines all possible solutions to the problem or program under consideration, and weighs the costs and benefits of each, so the decision maker can choose the best one. This rational-planning approach, said Lindblom, is "of course impossible.... It assumes intellectual capacities and sources of information that men simply do not possess, and it is even more absurd as an approach to policy when the time and money that can be allocated to a policy problem is limited, as is always the case."[1]

By contrast, the branch method, which Lindblom proposed "to clarify and formalize," is the method of making successive limited comparisons in order to adjust policy at the margins. According to Lindblom, this method is best suited to policymaking in democracies. It is unfortunate, he added, that "the literatures of decision-making, policy formulation, planning, and public administration formalize the first approach rather than the second, leaving public administrators who handle complex decisions in the position of practicing what few preach." Although Lindblom called muddling through a science, it was with tongue in cheek. The point is that policymaking in government is dynamic. It is an art form. Judgment, skill, and timing in the jockeying by stakeholders in budgeting and other decision processes determine what happens on a particular policy issue. Moreover, once a policy is made, it rarely stays made; goals constantly need to be tended and amended.

My reason for discussing Lindblom's views here is to compare this incremental or branch method with theories emphasized in microeconomics that reflect the root method. A revealing illustration of the difference between these two methods for governmental budgeting was played out in President Lyndon Johnson's effort in the mid-1960s to remake the budget process in the style of microeconomics by establishing what was called the "planning-programming-budgeting system," abbreviated as PPB.

The PPB System

The PPB idea, borrowed from systems analysis in the private sector, was applied by Robert S. McNamara, former president of Ford Motor Co., who was appointed by President Kennedy as secretary of defense. McNamara and his staff of "whiz kids" used systems analysis to compare alternative weapon systems. Their goal in doing this was to increase the leverage of the secretary in relation to the individual armed services. Before the Vietnam War escalated, McNamara was riding high. In 1965, President Johnson decided that because of his success, McNamara's approach should be applied not just in the defense sector, but across the board in government.

In an executive order issued in August 1965, Johnson in characteristically ebullient fashion directed all federal agencies to apply the PPB approach to the entire budget process. Federal agencies were to prepare planning documents and then issue analytical papers backing up their budget recommendations to the Bureau of the Budget. (This was before the bureau was reorganized and renamed the Office of Management and Budget in 1970.) In this process, they were supposed to identify program objectives and then subject different methods of fulfilling them to systematic comparison. Formally, this process was to consist of three kinds of reports prepared by each agency: *program memoranda*, describing the agency's strategy and comparing the cost and effectiveness of major alternative programs; *special analytic studies*, examining current and longer-run issues; and *program and financial plans*, summarizing program choices in terms of their outputs and costs, usually for a five-year period.

The experience of PPB was, to say the least, disappointing. The paper did not flow, or else it overflowed. Federal agencies used familiar bureaucratic stratagems to continue to operate the budget process in the way they were used to doing it. In some cases, they simply did not submit the required planning memoranda and analysis documents. Agency officials and often also the staff of the Budget Bureau in these cases operated as if nothing had changed. In other cases, agencies used the tactic of swamping the Budget Bureau with thick planning documents and elaborate issue papers that few if any high officials of the submitting agency had ever seen. Documents were sometimes sent to the bureau in cardboard boxes containing material that could not possibly have been read, much less thoughtfully considered, by top agency officials.

A little over three years after President Johnson established the government-wide PPB system, President Nixon quietly issued a memorandum abolishing it that began: "Agencies are no longer required to . . ." and then summarized the steps of the PPB system. Budget expert Allen Schick, in an article on this little-noticed event, pointed out, "No mention was made in the memo of the three initials which dazzled the world of budgeting when the PPB system was announced."[2]

Economist Charles Schultze, himself an accomplished inner and outer in the federal government, was a central figure in this story of the planning-programming-budgeting system. As director of the Budget Bureau when PPB was put in place, he was at the forefront of these efforts to apply microeconomics in government. After leaving the Johnson administration, Schultze discussed his experience in trying to implement PPB in a series of lectures at the University of California.[3] The lectures are a fascinating retrospective on the application of the root method to governmental policymaking.

Schultze explicitly indicated sympathy with Lindblom's argument about the difficulty of specifying the objectives of every possible public policy alternative and comparing them according to the degree to which they achieve their objectives. Digging into Lindblom's idea about muddling through, Schultze concluded that the PPB approach needed to adapt to the political process. In fact, he said, this is what actually happened under President Johnson. According to Schultze, "program planning and evaluation staffs in the agency head's immediate office, created by the PPB system, strengthen the role of the agency head in relations with the operating units."[4] The legacy of PPB in this case was that it made policy analysts — who tended to be new agency staff members — players in government policymaking. They become a permanent force, adding an analytical dimension to budgeting. They were empowered. Although not customarily discussed in these terms, this is what all budget reforms are all about — *power*. Budgeting became more analytical, but it didn't change all that much. It was still, and still is, an inherently political process.

The PPB system is not the only such effort by government reformers to make government decision making more rational by empowering people who engage in this style of thinking. There have been several similar reforms since PPB. Under President Carter in the late 1970s, the aim of applying what Lindblom called "the root method" to governmental budgeting was advanced under the highly publicized banner of "zero-based budgeting" (ZBB). This approach, as its name implies, required that every budget decision be made as if it were a new decision at ground zero, with planners systematically evaluating all the options for pursuing the contemplated purposes, not just examining how to adjust existing policies or programs at the margin. Earlier on, in the Nixon years, a similar reform had been advanced called "management by objectives" (MBO). Both Nixon's MBO system and Carter's ZBB system, like PPB before them, called for new processes, players, and documents and both bit the dust unceremoniously. Still, they added to PPB's legacy of empowering policy analysts in decision making.

A political scientist who played a major role in both interpreting and influencing public budgeting, Aaron Wildavsky, published in 1964 a widely read book calling all of these budget "reforms" into question. He argued that, despite assertions to the contrary, most budget decisions are *incremental.*[5] Each year, he said, decision makers look at what is being spent and decide how much to add to each account, sometimes making changes in the way programs work, but rarely if ever deeply analyzing whether the program is justified. This is the way it is, claimed Wildavsky, who documented his conclusion with detailed observations of federal budgetary decision making.

Fifteen years after the first edition of Wildavsky's book on the politics of the budgetary process was issued, he published a new version that boldly announced a further evolution in his thinking. He began by noting that his original book on the budgetary process had been written to show that the "accepted paradigm does not describe either how budgetary decisions are made or how they might be made." Now he said he wanted to go further: "This third edition claims (how well the reader will have to judge) that putting objectives first, alternatives second, and choices third is inefficient as a method of calculation, ineffective in relating thought to action, and inappropriate as a design for learning."[6] Specifically referring to PPB and Carter's zero-based budgeting system, in what I think was an exaggeration, Wildavsky asserted: "Rational choice (it is always right to be rational) limits calculations so choice can be made, uses history to correct mistakes, harnesses power through organizational incentives, and never, never ranks objectives or resources alone but always together."[7] PPB and ZBB, said Wildavsky, are the opposite of this; they represent, in his terms, "*Irrational* Policy Analysis."[8]

Where Do New Ideas Come From?

Although much of what happens in government policymaking is incremental in the way just described, new ideas do enter the governmental process. In the mid-1980s, a study on how new ideas enter the governmental process was conducted by political scientist John W. Kingdon.[9] His study consisted of interviews with elected and appointed officials of the federal government and career officials and people outside government from interest groups, the media, and academe. In all, Kingdon interviewed 247 people who were involved in health and transportation policymaking from 1976 to 1979. His framework for the analysis and nomenclature are both interesting and useful.

Kingdon's focus was on what he called "policy entrepreneurs," whom he defined as people who operate in three streams that flow into "the policy process," those concerning problems, policies, and politics. When the three streams converge, the result can be major policy changes. Kingdon said "focusing events" cause these convergences to occur, often in ways that are unpredictable, at moments when "policy windows" are open, allowing policy entrepreneurs to build coalitions to change policy in major ways. Kingdon's most important findings comport with what has been said so far about the role of appointed officials. "If any one set of participants in the policy process is important in the shaping of the agenda, it is elected officials and their appointees, rather than career bureaucrats or nongovernmental actors."[10] Compared with elected and appointed officials, Kingdon said, interest groups are important, but more in the way of blocking than originating policy changes. He found academics, policy researchers, and consultants to be important actors too, although generally in shaping policy alternatives.

Notes

1   Charles E. Lindblom, "The Science of 'Muddling Through'," *Public Administration Review* 19 (Spring 1959): 80.

2   Allen Schick, "A Death in the Bureaucracy," in eds. C. Albert Hyde and Jay M. Shafritz, *Government Budgeting: Theory, Process, Politics* (Oak Park, IL: Moore, 1978) p. 191.

3   Chatles L. Schultze, *The Politics and Economics of Public Spending* (Washington, D.C.: Brookings Institution, 1968).

4   Ibid., p. 94.

5   Aaron Wildavsky, *The Politics of the Budgetary Process* (Boston, MA: Little, Brown & Company, 1962), p. 13, emphasis added.

6   Aaron Wildavsky, *The Politics of the Budgetary Process* third edition (Boston, MA: Little, Brown & Company, 1979), p. v.

7   Ibid., p. v.

8   Ibid., p. vi., emphasis added.

9   John W. Kingdon, *Agendas, Alternatives, and Public Policies* (Boston, MA: Little, Brown & Company, 1984).

10   Ibid., p. 20.

5

Policy
Implementation

G etting an idea adopted is by no means the whole of the matter. In American government, because there is so much bargaining and jockeying about virtually every public policy, participants tend to get worn out once a new policy is adopted, and as a result do not follow up on what happens to policies after they are made. Moreover, participants in public policy-making are likely to be engaged in making other policies that also involve incessant bargaining and jockeying, so that even if they cared about what happened to a policy just made, they would be too preoccupied with other issues to have the time and energy to do much about it. *In a phrase, policy-making in America pushes out its own implementation.* For appointed officials inside of government who aspire to be effective managers, this creates outstanding opportunities. This point is made even more telling by virtue of the fact that public policies once they are made almost never (and this is no exaggeration) are so clear and precise that they are self-executing.

The bottom line is that policy is made in its execution. The attentive agency manager has a virtual cornucopia of opportunities to make a mark by working hard on policy implementation, which is the subject of this chapter. Doing this, however — that is, overseeing policy implementation — is no easy trick. There are pitfalls, complexities, and always some interests (especially internal to government) that are paying attention and can thwart the leader's wishes about how a particular policy should be executed.

There are two main barriers to policy implementation. One is the sheer size and complexity of the institutions the leader must deal with in any managerial endeavor in modern society. The second barrier is more subtle. It involves the tendency for some (although not all) of the people the leader must deal with inside government to "complexify." They may, for example, introduce mumbo jumbo about how hard it is to measure the things that public policies are supposed to achieve. This kind of internal positioning can be carried to the point that it wears down even the most well intended appointed official who wants to make a mark as a good manager. Don't let this happen to you!

A caveat is needed here: I am not saying that all of the people you must deal with inside of government in a particular policy network will try to undermine you as a policy manager. Quite to the contrary. As one successful state commissioner of human services recently told me, "Officials are fired by their subordinates." What he meant is that unless an appointed agency leader works well and honestly with the key people in career jobs inside the agency, he will be defeated in the end by his own staff.

Policy implementation involves seemingly logical steps, but they are not as definitive or straightforward as they may seem to be on the surface. Regulations must be written, interpreted, and put into effect once a law is passed. However, the way the organizations that are supposed to be affected by these regulations (be they public bureaucracies, private corporations, or nonprofit organizations) behave is not simply a matter of doing what the regulations say. There are games people play and many subtle ways that executing entities can go in directions and act in ways that contort and even undermine the goals of an appointed official seeking to manage the policy implementation process. These are not devious acts so much as they involve different preferences and ideas in interpreting laws, regulations, and policy directives. The challenge to the conscientious appointed leader inside America's governments is to put forward policy goals clearly and strongly and then follow up on them in steady and smart ways.

At their roots, new policies represent efforts to change the behavior of large organizations. They are important only if they do so. No matter how well crafted a public policy, how pure its intent, unless the policy is carried out, all is for naught. This process of converting "good" intentions in government into "good" results for citizens is an important basis on which the public should judge the performance of leaders in America's governments. In the poem "The Hollow Men" T. S. Eliot wrote:

> Between the idea
> And the reality
> Between the motion
> And the act
> Falls the Shadow

It is in this shadowland of policy implementation that appointed officials in government must shine a bright light and do what is often their most important work.

Implementation as Exploration

The first piece of advice for appointed leaders who care about policy implementation is to get out and about. There are few things as harmful to good management in government as spending all or most of one's time in Washington, Albany, or Sacramento. The world of distant observation deadens sensitivity to the work tens of thousands of state and local government employees and myriad nonprofit and for-profit organizations do at the ground level. This is not to say that the leader must grapple personally with all the details of implementing public policies and micromanage them. That would drive you nuts. The point is that unless the leader has a keen sense of what occurs at ground level, it is very hard to provide wise policy direction at the top. There is also a public-relations aspect to this advice about getting out and about. Not only do appointed leaders need to develop a "feel" for ground-level administration, it is also good to be seen doing so. You signal in this way that you are watching, and that you are aware of more than just the abstract discussions in Washington or the state capital.

A chapter in a book published in 1984 on policy implementation by Aaron Wildavsky and Angela Browne included a three-word sentence that encapsulates the point of this chapter. *"Implementation is exploration."*[1] To reiterate a point made earlier, public policy to a very high degree is made in the process of carrying it out. Appointed leaders in government are in the catbird seat for policy implementation, but to succeed they must be alert to the constant changes in policy that occur in implementation processes. Moreover, influencing the implementation process is not something one can do just at the beginning of a new program. It takes constant vigilance. How does the appointed leader do this and maintain sanity?

Textbooks on American government often define away this role for the top leaders in government by drawing a distinction between making policies and carrying them out. They depict the first of these tasks (making policy) as political, whereas the second task (policy implementation) is depicted as a ministerial job of civil servants whose role it is to take charge of policies once they are agreed to and do the things necessary (write regulations and exercise oversight) to put them into effect. Nice as it might be to adopt such a simple distinction, the fact of the matter is that most public policies are deliberately vague, and their purposes change frequently. Different elected and appointed leaders state policy goals in different ways, often as a part of their efforts to assemble the necessary political coalition to get a new policy adopted. A key legislator, for example, is likely to put a different spin on policy goals depending on the audience being addressed. Leaders of interest groups know this well. It is not unusual for them to try to influence management processes in a way that enables them to change the very purposes of governmental actions.

In sum, oversight for implementation by appointed officials has to be strategic, constant, and politically astute. The higher up you go in government, the less realistic it is personally to exercise such oversight. The way an appointed official relates to others, particularly people inside the bureaucracy and staff, to oversee policy implementation is as good an indicator as any for sorting out skillful policy managers from those who are not serious about this role.

Advice for Policy Managers

Three pieces of advice are critical to policy implementation. Number one, the leader and members of the leader's staff need to be *tuned in to organizational structures*: What agency or office is doing, or supposed to do, what part of the management job? What mindset does this organization have? Is it in sync with the policy goals the leader wants to achieve? The second piece of advice is, *Follow the money.* Know the budget allocations that are critical to a policy's implementation. Participate in the budget game. The third piece of advice is to *assess in-*

centives for getting organizations to do what they are supposed to do, or more specifically, what you would like them to do.

These three elements come together in the mundane business of acquiring and using information about what happens to policies after they are made. The fact of the matter is that appointed leaders in government cannot know everything about every policy's implementation. One important reason this is so is because many management jobs in government are carried out by *indirection*. That is, they are carried out by agents — state governments as agents of the federal government, local governments as agents of the states, and nonprofit organizations and private companies operating under contracts with states and localities.

Appointed officials have to be clear about the types of feedback information that realistically can be obtained in the fluid and complex environment of American federalism. (Key characteristics of American federalism are described in the appendix to this chapter.) If an official is responsible for national parks, for example, feedback and oversight clearly can and should be federal. However, for the great majority of U.S. domestic programs, the level for policy execution is sometimes the state, and more often localities and local communities. Trying to micromanage centrally for activities that are performed way down in the governmental food chain can be a source of great frustration.

Another way to summarize what is involved here for the operation of American federalism is that all governmental activities have *three dimensions* — setting policies, paying for them, and carrying them out. A health program can have national goals, be partially paid for by the federal government, and be administered by a state government or a local consortium of hospitals and health clinics. The key to exercising oversight is knowing what level of government or institution has *preponderate* responsibility. If the national government sets general goals and pays part (but not most) of the costs of a given service and does not administer that service directly, it is not realistic to expect federal officials to know everything about every aspect of its implementation and its effects. In a nutshell, managerial oversight has to be carried out in ways that reflect who's in charge. The questions asked have to be tailored to the authority of the political actors asking them. In a program area or for a service where the federal government's role is limited, oversight has to be broad and should not reflect misguided notions about micromanagement.

Reporters are notorious in demanding information in a way that misunderstands this reality of American federalism. Yet when a conscientious appointed official tries to set them straight, a common response is to regard that official as engaging in bureaucratic doubletalk intended to fend off responsibility. Unfortunately, the failure to face up to this dilemma and deal with accountability questions candidly and intelligently feeds public resentment toward government.

What Works?

Over the years, there have been fads about public management that have at their roots the desire to make decisions about governmental activities on the basis of the appealing test, *What works?* The point is made that the ultimate criterion should not be whether a given policy was carried out on a step-by-step basis as intended, but whether it made a difference for the people or groups it was supposed to affect. This idea is expressed in proposals to *"manage for results."* Unfortunately, some of these proposals reflect the kind of mumbo jumbo I referred to earlier as a potential stumbling block to conscientious appointed officials who want to influence policy implementation.

In 1993, the U.S. Congress actually enacted a law requiring the federal government on an across-the-board basis to manage for results. Called the Government Performance and Results Act (the "Results Act" for short), this act set up procedures for assessing and scoring the performance of all federal agencies. House of Representatives Majority Leader Dick Armey stated the purpose of the law as follows in a letter he sent to the director of the Office of Management and Budget in the Executive Office of the President. The Results Act, he said, is "designed to systematically provide Government decision-makers and the public with reliable information on what actual results federal programs and activities are achieving — i.e., what is working, what is wasted, what needs to be improved, and what needs to be rethought."[2] Under the terms of the Act, every agency must submit a plan to the Office of Management and Budget setting out its goals and indicating specifically how they will be achieved.

Regrettably for its authors, the new law got off to a bad start. A special task force of House of Representatives staff members set up to monitor this process gave numeric scores to all of the agency plans initially submitted by federal agencies under the act. Plans were scored according to ten factors, with up to ten points awarded for each, so that, along with a possible 5-point bonus, the best-performing agency could receive a score of 105. The highest score assigned to an agency in this review was 62, that for the Social Security Administration. The lowest score was 6.5, given to the Labor Department.

What stands out here in this example is that the Social Security Administration has *preponderate* responsibility for administering the programs under its jurisdiction. No wonder it got a high score. In sharp contrast, the Labor Department carries out almost all of its programs by indirection (that is, through grants-in-aid to states and localities that pay for part, often much less than a majority share, of a given training or employment program). Other agency scores ranged from 60 to 11. The mean score was 26.5.

Representative Armey's conclusion was hopeful but concerned. "Much remains to be done," he said, adding that these scores "illustrate rather starkly how far agencies are from the ideal."[3] Reports from the U.S. General Accounting Office (GAO) were less upbeat. GAO maintained that "examples of substantial performance improvements were relatively few, and many agencies did not appear to be well positioned to provide in 1997 a results-oriented answer to the fundamental Results Act question: What are we accomplishing?"[4] Repeatedly, the General Accounting Office pointed out that one of the main barriers to implementing the 1993 Results Act is the difficulty of measuring results for "programs that deliver services to taxpayers through third parties, such as state and local governments."[5] And that, of course, isn't all. A very large number of domestic social services are performed under contracts with literally hundreds of thousands of nonprofit and for-profit private-sector organizations.

As stated earlier, this discussion about government by indirection is by no means a small point. There is a plethora of situations in which federal grants-in-aid are made to a lower level of government or to some other entity where the grant or a contract pays a minor part of the costs of a given governmental function or activity. The same point applies even more strongly to state governments where a state provides seed money to publicize and stimulate certain kinds of local or community actions. In all of these situations in American government where higher levels of government (national and state) do not pay the piper, they cannot call the tune. They are not in a position to "manage for results." It is not wise to obligate them to collect detailed ground-level data in a way that assumes that they can exercise detailed, close oversight in a situation where they cannot do so.

An Example

Take as an example a federal grant-in-aid for a pilot program for intensive reading remediation for high school students. A school in a suburb may spend the same amount of money per student for this program as a school in a distressed urban neighborhood, and yet reading scores in the suburb may be much higher than in the city. Does this mean the students in the suburb performed better as a result of the federal grant-in-aid for the intensive reading remediation program? Not necessarily. In the case of a distressed urban area, one has to take into account the fiscal situation and also environmental conditions that make it harder to teach kids there to read. Overall, elementary and secondary education is primarily a state and local responsibility carried out by local school districts, and in the final analysis by schools and schoolteachers. Federal financial aid in this area is minor — less than 7 percent of total public elementary and secondary school spending.

There are several ways we can ask for feedback about the results we want school districts and schools to achieve in the case above. We can ask, what activities were funded with federal money? This is a *process* evaluation. We can also try to measure what are called *outputs*: How many students passed a particular reading test? The next level of results, as discussed below, is the hardest of all, involving *outcomes* — i.e., the measurement of whether a given program made a difference for the aided students.

Stipulate for illustrative purposes that there are several different types of aided school districts in this pilot reading remediation program, some in distressed urban areas and others in wealthy suburbs, and that both use the same special remediation curriculum for the same grade-level of students. Federal officials want to know if the curriculum worked. A research expert is called in, and is likely to say that what is needed is a control group that enables decision makers to get at the *"counterfactual."* What would have happened in the absence of the intensified reading remediation program? Moreover, the best way to do this is by conducting a social experiment in which some students in the different types of school districts receive the special reading curriculum and others do not, and then compare the results between the two groups. The preferred research method for conducting such social experiments is randomly to assign some students in each of the piloted school districts to a treatment group, and some to a control (non-treatment) group, and then observe the differences in their reading performance. That can provide the basis for answering the hard questions: Did the money spent on the intensified remediation curriculum make a difference? By how much? Where?

Unfortunately, social experiments are very hard to do, take a long time to conduct, and are very expensive. Governments can't do rigorous, formal evaluations of everything they pay for. It is in areas like this where overly elaborate aspirations about measuring the impact of government programs run the risk of scaring off conscientious officials from doing things — smart, sensible things — to hold government and its agents accountable. Policy officials should not attempt rigorously to ascertain the outcome of every dollar of government spending. What they should do is conduct social experiments *very selectively*. They should use this most rigorous random-assignment methodology for program evaluations to produce benchmarks for assessing programs, not to attempt to measure the results of every program scientifically. Using the example just given, we would like to be able to argue that if students in a particular reading program with certain kinds of characteristics score above a certain reading level, that program is likely to have produced that result. In short, what is needed, if something positive is to come out of the widely touted "performance-results movement," is a healthy dose of *realism*.[6]

Being an Accountable Leader

While it is less grand, there also is a practical, less rigorous way to use feedback about policy implementation for purposes of holding government agencies accountable. An appointed official can select certain politically important goals that, although they may not be definitive or scientifically derived, reflect what that leader cares about and wants to use as the basis for motivating government agencies and their agents in a given program area.

The key idea here is that this oversight approach is *motivational*. Procedures for overseeing and ratcheting up the achievement of the designated goals need to be clearly enunciated and frequently applied. This requires that the accountable leader meet regularly and work closely with the responsible line managers, using understandable data and data formats. How are the responsible line managers doing relative to program-wide averages and/or the performance of counterpart agencies, offices, or organizations? Regular give-and-take dialogues should be carried out in ways that take into account differences in conditions that can cause differences in what an agency or office can achieve as an essential part of such a motivational oversight process.

In this setting, the accountable leader can reward success by giving credit for it through awards and commendations. The leader can also bring other incentives to bear, such as promotions and bonuses (where this can be done) and opportunities for advanced training and networking that are career enhancing for high-performing program directors and their aides and associates. Regularly published report cards also can be used as a tool for achieving performance goals.

Or if the desired results fall short, the leader can use oversight dialogues to discuss actions that hopefully will produce better results at the next review. When it is necessary, steps can be taken (although often not easily) to shift administrative responsibilities and reassign low-performing personnel. Other less assertive motivational techniques can be used, for example, calling attention to ways to achieve better performance, showcasing productive processes and innovations, and just patiently talking through how changes can be made

In sum, much can be achieved by the accountable leader using low-key, but intensive and regular, hands-on motivational tactics in working relationships with implementing officials at the level of government that is *predominantly* responsible for the implementation of a given policy. Experts in public management, researchers, and systems analysts can aid the leader in selecting and using the best data sources as benchmarks for this purpose. But policy officials need to be careful not to be taken in by overly ambitious performance-management and evaluation approaches. In the final analysis, the ideas of experts can't be a substitute for wise and common-sensical attention to implementation on the part of appointed officials who are willing to be held accountable for *results*.

Notes

1   Browne, Angela, and Aaron Wildavsky, "Implementation as Exploration (1983)," in *Implementation*, Jeffrey L. Pressman and Aaron Wildavsky, eds. (Berkeley: University of California Press, 1984), p. 254. Italics added.

2   Armey, Dick, Letter to Franklin D. Raines, "*RE: Results Act Implementation*," Aug. 7, 1997

3   Ibid.

4   U.S. General Accounting Office, "*Managing for Results: Prospects for Effective Implementation of the Government Performance and Results Act*," (Washington, D.C.: June 3, 1997) GAO/T-GGD-97-113, p.5.

5   Ibid., p. 11.

6   For a longer discussion of the author's views, see *Social Science in Government: The Role of Policy Researchers* (Albany, NY: The Rockefeller Institute Press, 2000).

Appendix to Chapter 5

American Federalism

A ppointed officials who work in the field of U.S. domestic public affairs must have a good understanding of American federalism. The U.S. Bureau of the Census surveys America's governments every five years in years ending in "2" and "7" — dates that are as far away as possible from the decennial census years. The *Census of Governments* describes the characteristics, finances, and personnel of all "governmental units." Their total number is huge.

To be classified as a government, an entity must possess three attributes — existence as an organized unit, governmental character, and substantial autonomy as defined by the Census Bureau. In 1997 the United States officially had 87,453 governmental units. With the exception of the federal government and the 50 state governments, the rest of America's governments are local. About half are general-purpose local governments. The rest have special purposes. In 1997, the category of general-purpose governments included 3,043 counties, 19,372 cities, and 16,629 towns and townships. The remaining local units are special-purpose governments, 13,726 school districts, and also other special-purpose districts for particular functions like firefighting (5,601), housing and community development (3,470), water supply (3,409), sewerage (2,004), hospitals (764), and air transportation (476).

Illinois had the most local governments (6,722) in 1997 and Hawaii the least (20). Most local governments in the United States are small. Half of all municipalities (called villages or boroughs in some states) have less than 1,000 people. One-quarter of all counties have populations under 10,000. The following are three cardinal characteristics of American federalism:

> *Fragmentation.* Since the U.S. has so many (almost 90,000) local governments, it is clear that Americans must like localism. They want to be part of a community, living with people like themselves.

> *Diversity.* A second striking characteristic of American federalism, especially pertinent for this chapter, is the diversity of local governmental arrangements. This refers to the ways local governments are organized both among and within states. States determine the role and structure of local governments, and their practices are not uniform. In some states, counties are the most powerful local units and have appreciable powers and functions. This is the case in Maryland, New York, and Cali-

fornia. Counties in other states have hardly anything to do, as in Massachusetts and Connecticut where they are little more than the boundaries for judicial districts. In some states, towns are more important than cities. New York State had 8,246 towns in 1997, of which 1,133 had more than 300,000 people; no other state has towns that are even close to that large.

➤ *Layering.* Not only does America have many and diverse local governments, they tend to be piled on top of each other. This adds to the challenge of officials in overseeing policy implementation. Most people live in multiple local jurisdictions and pay taxes to several local governments, often with little idea of which local governments are receiving their tax money and for what purposes. An urban resident can live in a city, within a town, within a county, within an independent school district, and also be a resident of special districts for particular services — all of which collect taxes in ways that can befuddle even the most conscientious citizen.

Most reformers don't like this crazy quilt of American political localism. They press measures to curb governmental proliferation and simplify and clarify lines of accountability. But there is also a contrary view that holds that the fragmentation and diversity of American federalism has its benefits. This is the so-called "public-choice" position, which says that having multiple governments provides more opportunities for more people to get involved in civic life. People who favor this position also argue that different-sized regions are needed for different public services, reflecting their varied scope for efficient administration. Transportation services, for example, tend to be provided regionally, with a much broader scope geographically than, say, police and fire protection.

Liberals concerned about the isolation of the poor in the core area of the largest cities understandably don't like the public-choice theory. Nevertheless, whatever one's opinion on conceptual issues such as this, the pattern of local governance just described is what exists. Appointed leaders in America's governments who want to influence policy implementation must understand the fragmented, diverse, and layered character of American federalism.

6 Dealing With the Media

A s an appointed high official in government, you must cultivate the press and always appear to be talking candidly to them. This is very hard to do because there is so much hype in public relations, and because there is so little time to get one's point across, especially on television. Telegenic elected leaders who are good at sound bites and have celebrity status often make government unpopular because of the way they play on people's emotions by talking down to the public. What is most irritating is that these leaders in many cases set the tone. Their simplistic and superficial treatment of issues does more than hurt their image. It demeans other people in government — both appointed and career officials — who are caring and hardworking in carrying out the day-to-day business of running America's governments. While all of this is true, as an appointed leader in government you have no choice. You have to deal with the press.

One of your biggest problems in government will be that you get publicity when you don't want it, and you can't get it when you do want it. Reporters seek controversy — better yet, a good fight. You get noticed if you take somebody on. It is not worth the trouble to try to find journalists with an audience for stories about successes in the day-to-day serious work of governing. Look at it from their side: The competition in the media for audience is immense. It is hard for journalists to get noticed with the ever-growing number of television channels, newspapers, magazines, radio stations, and web sites — a virtual cornucopia of information outlets. Here are ideas for dealing with the press.

> ➤ *Maintaining your image and making it as good as you possibly can is one of the hardest and subtlest challenges you will face as an appointed official in government.* Some reporters are not going to like what you are doing, seeing it as too conservative, too liberal, or just not what they think you should do. While they may profess and believe that they adhere to high standards of journalistic objectivity, after a while bad relationships develop if the chemistry is just plain wrong. The higher up you go in government and the more visible you become, the more likely it is that such personal animosities will emerge. Where there are weaknesses in your record and vulnerabilities in your performance (and there are bound to be some), the reporter who has it in for you will find them. Since this can happen, you need to be scrupulous in protecting your reputation and

preserving your integrity. In fact, the bolder you are in trying to change policies or win the adoption of new policies, the more likely this advice will be essential to your success as a government official.

➤ *Some adversaries you acquire along the way in government should be treated deferentially, some not so deferentially.* These are basically two different groups. Some adversaries will never be anything else. Having them on the other side even can be helpful to you. Other adversaries will be adversaries one day and friends the next. The attack mode should be reserved for the first group.

➤ *Care about your style.* If you are shrill and always hurling lightning bolts, you may, as the expression goes, get ink, but you won't get respect. The saying, "I don't care what they say about me as long as they spell my name right," is not good guidance.

➤ *Calls from prominent reporters should get your quick personal attention.* The higher you go in government, the more likely it is you will have a press assistant. Still, there is no substitute for taking and making press calls yourself when a subject you are working on is very timely. This is because the news is perishable, and also because reporters care about hearing things in your own voice and being able to ask you questions.

➤ *There is a corollary to this: You don't need to be accessible all the time.* If you don't want to answer certain questions, don't take calls from reporters who are likely to ask them. "No comment" is a bad answer, and generally speaking going off the record is dangerous.

➤ *News cycles are inexorable.* If you don't get back right away to reporters who call you, it may not be worth it, or even necessary, to do so. If you miss their news cycle, you can't easily create a new one. On the other hand, for most other callers, even important ones, the time line is not so short.

➤ *When you talk to a reporter or do a television interview, be prepared!* Practice interviews for television, even out loud. Get some coaching. Know what to wear and how to hold your hands and use gestures. Above all, know what your message is and stick to it. Bend each answer to the questions you are asked in order to present and stress your message.

➤ *Limit your answers to reporters' questions (especially on television) to three or four key points.* Avoid clutter. Use understandable examples to make important points — examples that reflect and relate to everyday experiences.

➤ *Play it straight.* Even at a loss of top billing, or of any billing at all, it is not smart to exaggerate so much that you distort the facts. (A little fact bending is okay, but don't overdo it.) The most respected journalists, the experts they respect, and the other people they use as sources know when you are playing fast and loose with the facts. Don't lower your standards for short-term gain. Maintain your integrity. Over the long haul this is the most precious currency of public relations, one that comes in very handy when there is a hot issue or controversy and you are caught right smack in the middle of.

➤ *Reporters like numbers.* A number is easy for them to use in a story because it is not something they can be criticized for misstating by their editors, readers, or viewers. Twenty-three point five percent of anything is easier to write about than how the governor treated her party chair or a legislative leader on a particular hot issue. Numbers can help you get a story out. We hit a target of "X." Someone missed a target of "Y." A certain program helped or hurt "Z" numbers of people. Your numbers can be compared with what someone else said, what went before, what some other state or city did.

➤ *Geography matters.* What you say depends on where you are. Information or ideas about where you are, which is always somebody's home state or city, are easy stories to tell and easy stories for reporters to write.

➤ *Reporters like stories that are counterintuitive.* These are stories that get their readers to say, "Gee, I didn't know that."

➤ *Pace yourself.* Don't talk to the press or go on television when you are tired. This applies to all public events. If you have an important appearance in the evening, don't go to the office in the morning. Take a nap. Metabolism matters. Members of the press are like vultures circling and watching all the time. That's their job. Don't make it too easy for them.

➤ *No matter how hectic things get, keep your perspective.* Know what you really care about and what you hope to achieve. Don't be diverted by every temptation for the limelight. You can't do or speak about everything. If someone else gets credit for something you care about but it is not your highest priority, here's one word of advice — *relax.*

7 Wielding Power in America's Governments

Appointed officials in America's governments serve "at the pleasure" of elected officials, often for relatively short periods of time, although frequently they are repeaters. In their capacity as leaders of agencies, departments, and commissions, appointed officials have substantial responsibility both for setting public policies and carrying them out. This is a challenging role. It often brings the satisfaction of performing public service in a way that reflects a commitment to important areas of public life and high ideals of citizenship. It can bring a heady feeling of power and responsibility, and also pave the way to future fame and fortune. Yet appointed leaders must always remember that power in a democracy is on loan. The terms of the loan, though rarely expressed in a clear and precise way, require good behavior and adherence to values and ideas that can win and hold popular support. The power of appointed officials is hard to delineate and hold on to under the best of circumstances, but it is downright perishable if you abuse the public trust. There are plenty of people watching you. This includes the politicians who appointed you and all their adversaries who have different purposes from yours. Other guardians are the ubiquitous mass media, interest groups, and the citizens you serve. All have access to instruments for curbing your power — or eliminating it.

Appointed officials can turn governments' purposes into results by setting and adjusting goals wisely and paying close attention to how they are carried out. But you will not succeed in the important and serious work of good government unless you are smart about the kinds of political realities this book seeks to impart. America's governments are fragmented, diverse, fast changing. American political pluralism, with its multiple actors and constant policy bargaining, can be brutal and unforgiving. The rough and tumble quality of deal making reflects an almost frontier-like spirit that resents people who have political power yet needs and respects its savvy exercise.

Nine Suggestions

The comment was made in the first chapter that the most important thing an appointed official manages is his or her career. There are no clear British or French types of routes to high office. You make your own way. By way of a summary, the nine suggestions below deal with key aspects for being a successful leader inside America's governments.

1. *At the end of the Clinton period, it is appropriate to begin this list by stressing that leaders are role models.* It is not just ideas, your administrative skills, and your politics that matter. The leader sets a tone. And it is not just an institutional tone. It is a moral tone about responsibility, country, family, respect for others, firmness but fairness. Bad personal traits undermine your effectiveness no matter how extensive your knowledge and how smart and canny you are in working with political groups and policy ideas.

2. *Care about partisanship.* Ultimately, the road to high office will label you politically and require you to pick and stick with a partisan label. Make a choice you can live with. This is not to say that being a Democrat means that you will never serve under a Republican or vice versa. There are times when elected officials see advantages in being non-partisan by relying on people of the opposition party in key posts. But this is more the exception than the rule.

3. *Always be mindful of the hyper-pluralism of American government and the great barrier reef of federalism, which can wreck voyages to accomplishment.* It is crucial for top officials to have a sophisticated understanding of the fragmented, diverse, and complex governmental environment in which you must operate.

4. *Cultivate the press.* The challenge involved in doing this is multifaceted — to be a straight shooter, to win

and hold respect, and at the same time to be interesting. You have to think carefully about which reporter to talk to and which not to call back, when to go on camera, and when not. You will need a smart press assistant for facilitating media contacts and writing announcements and press releases that will get attention amid the din of voices in public affairs. But in the final analysis your image and public persona have to be of your own making.

5. *Be careful about confidences*. It is important to have trusted associates, but trust has its limits. The political world changes all the time, so there are bound to be situations in which, much as you would like to do so, you cannot rely on people you like and admire to do what you want or to work with you in the way you want them to. Understand this. This also means that in the periods of the most intense political maneuvering your most cherished values and your private opinions of others should be kept to yourself.

6. *Be careful about jokes*. That funny remark that shows how somebody erred or how their personality is flawed may be hilarious, but jokes have a way of backfiring. The critical distinction is between gracious humor (often a nice touch) and sarcasm. Sarcasm is dangerous in public life.

7. *Pace yourself*. Conserve your energy so you are fresh for major confrontations, speeches, and meetings. This is timing in the short term. A good sense of tim-

ing in the long term is also necessary. You need to think about when to act and when to wait. Patience does not come easily to people who are action oriented, which is an essential quality for accomplishing things in government. In big bureaucracies where delays are endemic, an appointed leader often sees his or her role as fighting against inertia. Nevertheless, patience is called for in those situations where letting the action come to you will give you more options, more scope for action, more power.

8. *Be consistent.* After awhile you can't change your image, so don't make the mistake of trying a lot of different personas and appearing to be highly unpredictable. Think about what you stand for and keep these thoughts in a mental file that you refer to often but that always stays locked.

9. *Think about your future.* Families have to eat. Kids have to go to college. There are limits to the options you have for considering how to move from being an inner to being an outer. Still, there are relationships you can cultivate so that at the right moment you can make the right transitions. In part, this advice involves your career choice: You need to have a base. You need to be a lawyer, doctor, professor, or business executive so you can take risks and serve on the typically short-term basis of appointive high-level leadership in America's governments. When you are young, you can and should try different roles in and

around government and politicians. However, you need to be thinking even then about developing a professional or industrial base as the area of your major activity and expertise if public service appeals to you. This is because appointive posts are time limited and inherently unstable either by your choice or by somebody else's.

Expanding the Talent Pool for Public Service

Because there is so little generalized understanding of appointive leadership in America's governments, people who might be interested in high-level appointive public service tend not to have a good understanding of the numbers, character, and roles of inners and outers. Therefore, many people interested in public service tend to learn about these roles when it is too late for them to set their sights on serving in them.

As a nation, we need to consider ways to increase the talent pool for appointive post despite the tendency at all levels of American government to be so focused on the moment that the officials who must be involved in the job of appointing people to leadership posts are unprepared when the time comes to form a new administration. As stated earlier, the common reaction on the part of the winners of major elections is to take a vacation at the end of what is bound to have been a hectic and frenetic campaign. Even when there is a changeover in administrations and a different political party takes office in the national or a state government, the transition process to assemble ideas and people for the new administration tends to be a short, frenetic period, crunched in between the election and the inauguration. It is a period when most of the key actors involved are exhausted and rest and recreation really are needed.

The American political system would be well served by institutionalizing processes that provide trustworthy, well-vetted information about candidates for high appointive office. Such institution building to broaden the talent pool for appointive office is hard to do for several reasons. One reason is because of the political litmus test involved — i.e., the need for people whose purposes, values, and party identification fit those of the appointing official. Another is that many appointed officials tend not to be known nationally because they operate in specialized areas. Knowledge of the people and politics in a particular functional area of activity is needed to determine who has administrative talent and political skills and might be available for a key leadership position inside government. Still another reason that it is hard to expand the supply of candidates for appointive public office is that the best candidates tend to take a deferential position (at least publicly), insisting that they do not seek office. Finally, salaries in the public sector, even for cabinet-level positions, tend to be lower than the salaries the best candidates can receive in the private sector or in leadership positions at large universities, foundations, and other nonprofit organizations, many of which perform services closely related to public services and that, in some cases, are funded under government contracts.

Based on the results of a 1998 survey of one thousand recipients of masters' degrees from five cohorts of graduates of thirteen graduate schools of public policy, public administration, and public affairs, Paul Light identified what he calls "the end of government-centered public service."

As opposed to government services, Light showed that many of the respondents in this survey chose challenging positions in nonprofit organizations or in the private sector. In the case of nonprofit organizations, their roles have grown so rapidly in recent years that, indeed, this trend can be thought of — not as privatization — but as the *"nonprofitization"* of public services. Light notes, as I have stressed in this book, that many of the people whose careers he studied move around among the public, private, and nonprofit sectors. His findings reinforce the argument and proposals advanced here about the importance of adopting measures to attract talented leaders, not for their whole careers, but for part of their career, to appointive leadership positions inside government in positions that are central to the operations of large sectors and institutions of our national life.[1]

Government service has a special appeal if the right people can be identified at the right time and the right signals and information can be given to them. Indeed, public service can be the experience of a lifetime. What is needed are improved ways to link appointing officials with qualified candidates. In the private sector, head-hunting firms fulfill this role, and it needs to be added are well paid for doing so. However, in the public sector there tends to be resistance to paying large fees (often half a person's first-year salary) to a head-hunting firm, even if firms exist to serve this market.

What is needed is inventive attention to ways to do institution building for purposes of preparing and using sophisticated dossiers about potential candidates for high appointive public office. This should include candidates outside the immediate geographical area of the appointing official and outside that official's circle of acquaintances, but who nonetheless have similar values and appear to have the right qualities for personal rapport. Such an institutional capability to increase the supply of candidates for appointive office would have an additional benefit. It would send a signal about the importance of locating talented candidates for leadership posts in the public service — people with demonstrated records of success who are ready for new challenges.

Often people who have made it in their chosen field feel they haven't repaid the society and the country for their success. There should be ways to network with such people that could open the door for them to accomplishment in the public service. Identifying good candidates, obtaining their consent to have their name put forward, and presenting a convincing case as to why they should be considered for a certain post requires time, money, and ingenuity. However, the stakes are high and the contributions people can make in the public service are important. Much would be gained from efforts to build institutional capacity in this way to assist both Republicans and Democrats.

Large public agencies occasionally do avail themselves of head-hunting services by private firms; and in a number of specialized areas, boutique head-hunting firms perform this role for particular functional areas of government. But this tends to be uncommon. This is despite the fact that universities and other large nonprofit organizations often contract with headhunting firms for search services on a basis that has many of the same characteristics as approaches used in the private sector.

A logical starting point for expanding the talent pool for appointive public service would be to have foundations convene a cross-section of former elected and appointed officials to consider how to organize, build, and support new institutional mechanisms to perform this role. Many questions would have to be answered: Would it be best to hire existing search firms or establish new ones? Would the best approach be to create hybrid organizations that would contract with existing search firms and experts on an as-needed basis? What kinds of head-hunting expertise is best suited to this role? How would a new administration or an appointing official engage such services? Would governments pay some portion of the costs? What guidelines should be used to set these fees?

The case for investing in this kind of institution building is a strong one. In saying this, I do not mean to gainsay the argument frequently made that there should be fewer appointed officials in America's governments. Many experts on public administration hold this view, as was pointed out earlier. However, there should be no argument about expanding the size and quality of the talent pool for high appointive office, given the special character of America's governments (like it or not) which involves relying heavily on people serving in these roles. Groups interested in reforming government could make a substantial contribution by helping to design and by supporting workable systems to identify and attract talented citizens for high-level appointive public service.

As a corollary to this, young people, especially students interested in the public service, should be encouraged to seek staff positions that enable them to obtain knowledge about the "real politics" of leadership in the American public sector. Just because a person interested in government is young does not mean people won't care about what that person does with her time and energy. If public service is an area of interest to a student in college or even high school, it is not too early to think about what that person might like to do in public life — both in the short run and over the longer term. When you are young, you can work closely with either or both elected and appointed political leaders to obtain valuable insights and experience. The reason for doing this should be to explore the "ins and outs" of possibly having a career that, over the course of one's professional life, includes being an "*inner and outer*" in America's governments.

Notes

1   Paul C. Light, *The New Public Service* (Washington, D.C.: Brookings Institution Press, 1999).